VHF radio
including GMDSS

an **RYA**_training_ publication

Updated 2004

D1078618

RYA

Published by
The Royal Yachting Association
RYA House Ensign Way Hamble
Southampton SO31 4YA
Tel: +44 (0)845 345 0400
Fax: +44 (0)845 345 0329
Email: info@rya.org.uk
Web: www.rya.org.uk

CONTENTS

INTRODUCTION

Over the past few years marine communications have been revolutionised by the introduction of the Global Maritime Distress and Safety System (GMDSS). Designed by the International Maritime Organisation and supported by the International Telecommunication Union, it ensures that ships anywhere in the world can communicate with a Rescue Co-ordination Centre on shore by two independent means without the need for a specialist radio operator.

Yachts and small craft are not bound to carry radio transmitters and receivers and are under no obligation to participate in GMDSS. However, any mariner who wants to communicate with other ships, harbour authorities and Rescue Co-ordination Centres, has no alternative but to keep reasonably up-to-date with the equipment and techniques of the commercial shipping world.

Some elements of the pre-GMDSS means of communication will continue to be available until 2005 but it will become increasingly important for the yachtsman to participate in the new system if he wants to be certain of the ability to send an effective distress message.

Cellular phone networks, although not originally designed for maritime use, have proved extremely effective in inshore waters where marine VHF was previously the only viable means of communication. Mobile phones are still no substitute for marine VHF as they lack the essential ability to participate in an open network or receive and transmit broadcast messages such as urgency and safety messages, but they can provide a point of entry into the shore phone network. They are so effective that coast radio stations are now rarely asked to provide link calls to the shore. Jersey Radio and some other stations abroad still offer the facility but mainland UK coast radio stations have now closed.

The continuing strength of maritime VHF is the facility to provide both discrete ship to ship or shore station conversations and broadcast messages.

With hundreds of thousands of users sharing just 59 international channels there have to be rules and procedures which are understood and followed by everyone. They don't have to be followed slavishly but if they are totally ignored, communication would be impossible.

The purpose of this book is to explain how boaters can join the international community of VHF marine radiotelephony, providing for their own safety without interfering with other users.

REQUIREMENTS AND REGULATIONS

THE REQUIREMENT

In order to fit or use radio equipment in any vessel the owner must take into account three different sets of regulations:

a) The equipment must be built to a type approval standard.

b) It must be covered by a valid radio licence; either a Ship Radio Licence or a Transportable Radio Licence, both renewable annually.

c) It must be operated only under the direct personal supervision of a holder of the appropriate Certificate of Competence and Authority to Operate.

Equipment Conformity

All radio equipment fitted in yachts must meet certain minimum performance standards. These ensure that sets operate effectively in a range of conditions and that they avoid interference to other users during rescue operations.

Marine radio equipment offered for sale in the UK must conform to the operational requirements of the Global Maritime Distress and Safety System (GMDSS) and the technical requirements of the European Radio Equipment and Telecommunications Terminal Equipment (R&TTE) Directive; otherwise it may not be licensed for use and could be subject to confiscation if used. Would-be buyers can check that sets are compliant by looking for the marks shown right.

All equipment, or the handbook accompanying it, should have a Declaration of Conformance stating that it meets the requirements of the R&TTE Directive. It should also have information on its intended use, including the countries of the EU in which it is intended that the equipment be used. Second-hand equipment or that bought overseas may not conform to the Directive and could be fitted with incorrect channels for UK operation. If you have any doubts about whether equipment conforms to the R&TTE directive, or is GMDSS compatible, consult Ofcom or the Maritime Coastguard Agency (MCA) before purchase. Their telephone numbers are: Ofcom: 0845 456 3000 and MCA: 023 8032 9100.

The RYA's website has some Frequently Asked Questions (FAQs) on marine radio on www.rya.org.uk/cruising and the Ofcom website has information on all radio regulations on www.ofcom.org.uk

Ofcom staff carry out regular inspections to ensure that any equipment used on UK registered vessels operates in conformity with the relevant technical parameters.

The ship radio licence

The Wireless Telegraphy Act of 1949 requires all vessels fitted with radio equipment to have a valid Ship Radio Licence which should be displayed prominently on the vessel. The licence costs £20 (in 2003) and is renewable annually. If your licence is not valid you could be fined and have your radio equipment confiscated.

The ship's licence covers any or all of the following for use on board the craft and its tender as long as they have been declared on the application form:

Digital Selective Calling (DSC) equipment associated with the GMDSS.

Medium frequency, high frequency and Marine VHF equipment.

Hand held marine VHF radios.

Satellite communications equipment (Ship Earth Stations).

Radar, including Search and Rescue Radar Transponders (SARTs).

Low powered on board communications equipment (including UHF and repeater stations).

Emergency Position Indicating Radio Beacons (EPIRBs) using 406MHz, 121.5 / 243MHz or 1.6 GHz.

A hand-held VHF radio must be covered by a Ship Radio Licence or licensed separately as a transportable unit. A transportable licence issued with a 'T' reference for recognition purposes, allows the hand-held radio to be used on any vessel regardless of the vessel's licence status. Those transportable sets equipped with Digital Selective Calling (DSC) have a Maritime Mobile Service Identity (MMSI) begining with the numbers 2359.

A unique call-sign which remains with the vessel through changes of both name and ownership, is issued to the vessel at the same time as the first Ship Radio Licence. The application form is also used to register details of a 406 MHz EPIRB and GMDSS compatible DSC radio or satellite communications equipment which require a Maritime Mobile Service Identity (MMSI). MMSIs are discussed in greater detail on page 13.

The application form asks for details of the owner, the vessel and the number and type of radios carried on board the vessel and its tender. A single licence fee covers any number of pieces of radio equipment; details are held on a database available to the Coastguard in an emergency.

Charities pay a concessionary licence fee. To qualify, they must produce a valid charity registration number and prove that their object is 'the safety of human life in an emergency'.

During office hours contact the following for an application form:

The Radio Licensing Centre
The Post Office
PO Box 1495
Bristol BS99 3QS

Website: www.radiolicencecentre.co.uk
Tel: 0870 243 4433
Fax: 0117 921 8444

Operator qualifications

To maintain operational standards and ensure knowledge of distress, emergency and safety procedures a maritime radio may only be operated by a holder of the appropriate Certificate of Competence and Authority to Operate or by someone under his direct personal supervision.

Certificate of competence

The certificate of competence required will vary according to the type of cruising area and radio apparatus used. Anyone wishing to cruise outside VHF range can get information about the relevant certificates of competence from the MCA, telephone 023 8032 9100.

In the majority of cases a Short Range Certificate (SRC) is all that is required and authority to conduct these examinations has been delegated to the Royal Yachting Association (RYA). All candidates are now assessed on knowledge of Digital Selective Calling (DSC) and GMDSS but are not required to have a knowledge of public correspondence procedures. Holders of the Restricted Certificate of Competence in Radiotelephony (VHF only) must be assessed for the SRC if they intend to use DSC equipment.

A list of recognised centres running SRC courses is available from the RYA, tel: 023 8062 7400 or website: www.rya.org.uk. Full details of the syllabus and form of examinations are contained in RYA book *G26 - VHF Radio- Short Range Certificate syllabus and sample exam questions*. There is no age limit for candidates.

An SRC may be obtained in the following ways:

1. For candidates *without* a Restricted Certificate of Competence in Radiotelephony (VHF only):

    a) by attending an eight hour assessed course at an RYA training centre.

    OR

    b) by taking a practical and written examination at an RYA training centre.

2. For candidates *with* a Restricted Certificate of Competence in Radiotelephony (VHF only):

    a) by attending a three to four hour assessed course at an RYA training centre.

    OR

    b) by taking a written and practical examination on the use of GMDSS organised by an RYA training centre.

The remaining VHF radiotelephones without DSC may be operated by holders of the Restricted Certificate of Competence in Radiotelephony (VHF only) but it is desirable to have a knowledge of the GMDSS.

Authority to operate

An Authority to Operate is issued at the same time as the Certificate of Competence. It may be granted to anyone age 16 or over. The Authority to Operate is the document which authorises the holder to operate a ship radio station on board a vessel entitled to fly the British flag. It may be suspended by the Secretary of State in the event of gross procedural error in which case the holder has the right to have the matter referred to an Advisory Committee.

Licences for yacht clubs, marinas etc.

Licences are available which permit Yacht Clubs, Marinas and similar organisations to establish a base station in the UK. Full details are given in Coastal Station Radio Information Sheet available from:

Ofcom,
Riverside House,
2a Southwark Bridge Road,
London SE1 9HA

Tel: 0207 981 3000

www.ofcom.org.uk

MANAGEMENT OF THE MARITIME MOBILE BAND

THE VHF INTERNATIONAL MARITIME MOBILE BAND

VHF frequencies between 156.00MHz and 174.00MHz are allocated to the Maritime Mobile Service (MMS); that is, for use by ships fitted with VHF radio. This allocation is made by international agreement to introduce order into what would otherwise be a chaotic situation.

The band is divided into 59 channels with spacing of 25kHz between each as listed in Annex C. In addition, national authorities allocate a number of private channels.

Simplex and duplex working

With simplex, the system found in virtually all leisure craft and small workboats, transmission is only possible in one direction at a time. Thus you can either transmit or receive but not both simultaneously. The single antenna is switched from receive to transmit and back again by means of the press-to-transmit switch.

Duplex transmissions are possible in both directions simultaneously. It needs two frequencies and generally two antennas or a special duplex filter.

Ship-to-shore working channels are allocated on a two-frequency basis; for example, Ch26 has two frequencies - the ship transmits on a frequency of 157.3MHz and the shore station transmits on 161.9MHz.

It is possible to use simplex equipment on the two frequency channels, but transmission is still only possible in one direction at a time. The press-to-transmit switch automatically selects the correct frequency for transmission or reception.

Semi-duplex working has simplex at one end and duplex at the other. It is virtually the same as simplex working but saves the duplex operator having to release his Press-to-Transmit switch. Two frequencies are required.

It's important to note that two ships are incapable of holding a conversation on duplex frequencies and therefore all inter-ship channels are simplex.

International channels

Each channel is allocated for one or more of eight specific purposes and it is important to select a suitable channel for your particular use:

1) Distress safety and calling

Channel 16 has always been the VHF Distress Safety and Calling frequency and is likely to remain so for the foreseeable future. The normal routine is to establish contact on Ch16 and arrange to move to a mutually acceptable working frequency as quickly as possible. However, the number of radio telephones in use is such that, in the busiest areas, there is great pressure on Ch16 and Rescue Centres fear that a distress call may be missed due to congestion. Although all ships are encouraged to maintain a continuous watch on Ch16 when at sea, callers are encouraged to use working frequencies for initial calls whenever possible; this can only be done if the station called is maintaining a listening watch on that frequency.

The introduction of DSC, discussed in more detail later, reduces congestion on Ch16 as the initial electronic alert is sent as a very short data burst using Ch70. This is why Ch70 must never be used for voice communication.

2) **Bridge-to-bridge**

Channel 13 is an inter-ship channel reserved exclusively for bridge-to-bridge communication on matters of navigational safety.

3) **Intership**

Channels 6, 8, 72 and 77 should be used for intership working as they are exclusively for that purpose. Other intership channels are allocated for additional purposes; for example Ch10 for pollution control and weather broadcasts, Ch9 by harbour pilots (see Annex C). Small craft should avoid using these channels.

4) **Port operations**

Channels 11, 12 and 14 are most commonly used for port operations but refer to a nautical almanac for local variations.

5) **Ship movements (very similar to port operations)**

Ship movements are often conducted on the single frequency channels such as **Ch15, 17 and 69**

6) **UK small craft safety**

Channel 67 is single frequency ship-to-ship and is used by HM Coastguard (HMCG) as the Small Ship Safety Channel in the UK only.

7) **Public correspondence**

Channels allocated for public correspondence use two frequencies and are now seldom used for link calls to shore. HM Coastguard is using some of them for weather forecasts and navigational warnings.

Private channels

A number of private channels, Simplex and Duplex, are allocated for national use. The MCA uses Ch0, to control distress and safety traffic. Others are allocated to organisations such as ferry companies and harbour tug operators for internal use. Sailing Schools may apply for a private channel for which a fee is payable. Certain frequencies outside the International Maritime Band can also be allocated for private use.

With the exception of ChM and M2 a normal Ship Radio Licence does not include the use of any of these private channels and unmodified radios fitted in small craft cannot receive them.

National variations

The International Telecommunications Union (ITU) permits national authorities to modify the international frequency allocation to suit local operating procedures. The main UK variations are:

Channel M, a private simplex channel on 157.85MHz, is one of two available to British yacht clubs for safety boats and race control. It is shown on some VHF sets as **P1 or 37**. A normal Ship Licence permits all craft to use this frequency, **but only in UK waters.**

Since yacht clubs are not fitted with Ch16 the initial call must be made on ChM if that is their listed working frequency.

Channel M2 is the other frequency available for use by British yacht clubs. It uses a simplex frequency of 161.425MHz and is included in UK ship licences. It is now the preferred channel for yacht race management but it may not be available on some older VHF equipment.

Channel 80 is a duplex channel for use by marinas and ships calling them. Since marinas are not fitted with Ch16 the initial call must be made on Ch80 if that is the listed frequency.

GMDSS

WHAT IS GMDSS?

In 1902 the introduction of Morse Code sent by radio from ships significantly reduced the number of shipping losses. However, nearly 100 years later there were still significant losses when a distress call was never made because there was no time or, if made, it went unheard. In order to address this continuing problem the International Maritime Organisation (IMO) introduced the Global Maritime Distress and Safety System (GMDSS).

The system requires that ships be fitted with equipment which ensures that a casualty can alert search and rescue organisations and other ships with the minimum of delay. Pressing a single red button can send a digital distress alert, which gives both the identity and the position of the casualty. The whole process takes about fifteen seconds.

GMDSS regulations are now compulsory for all commercial vessels over 300grt, registered fishing vessels and craft carrying 13 or more passengers. These are called 'compulsory fit vessels'. Some smaller commercial vessels are strongly advised to fit VHF DSC.

As DSC equipment is being fitted on small craft it is planned that Convention (IMO member) ships will be permitted to cease a listening watch on Ch16 after 1 February 2005. Until then Ch16 must be monitored in order to receive emergency traffic. Thereafter, it may only be possible to communicate with these ships on Ch13, the bridge-to-bridge frequency.

Although HM Coastguard will continue to listen to Ch16 at its stations, after 2005 it will cease to have an operator whose sole job it is to monitor the channel. The only way to guarantee communications with all authorities within VHF range is by fitting VHF/DSC. Pleasure craft are counted as 'voluntary fit' and may fit any component of the GMDSS.

Compulsory fit craft must be fitted with:

- VHF DSC marine radio (and MF/HF DSC if in areas other than A1)
- 406 MHz Emergency Position Indicating Radio Beacon
- Search and Rescue Radar Transponder
- Radar
- Navtex
- Waterproof hand held VHF Radio

GMDSS areas

The world has been divided into four GMDSS areas and the radio equipment that merchant ships must carry depends on the sea areas in which they trade. The areas in NW Europe are shown in *Fig 3.1* below.

Sea area A1

Within range of shore-based VHF coast stations fitted with DSC (30 to 50 miles, depending upon height of aerial).

Sea area A2

Within range of shore-based MF/HF coast stations fitted with DSC (100 to 300 miles).

Sea area A3

Within the coverage area of INMARSAT satellites (between 70°N and 70°S).

Sea area A4

The remaining sea areas using HF DSC.

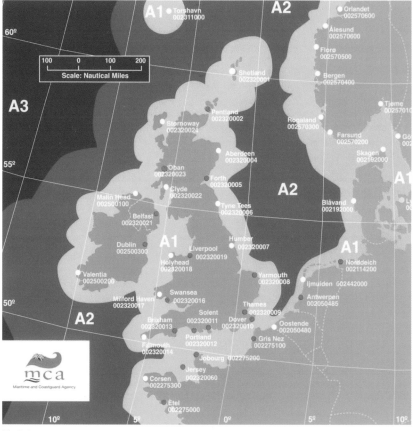

Fig 3.1

MARINE VHF AND DIGITAL SELECTIVE CALLING EQUIPMENT

FITTING VHF

Position

The radiotelephone is usually located in the cabin of a small boat. It should be securely fastened, in a convenient position clear of spray and dampness, away from the engine and any heat source. The set is connected to the yacht's power supply (observing the correct polarity) with the antenna feeder cable connected. No earth is needed. A waterproof extension loudspeaker, sited close to the steering position allows the helmsman to monitor the radio without disturbing crew who may be sleeping.

Power Supplies

While receiving, the radio consumes very little current. While transmitting, the current may rise to five or more amps. Generally, transmissions are infrequent and unlikely to present a serious drain on the boat's battery. However, some thought should be given to the need to send a distress message if the vessel were sinking and the main battery flooded. Under these circumstances a hand-held radio with its own internal battery is very desirable.

Antennas

The high gain antenna is about two metres long and concentrates the radiated power along a narrow horizontal beam giving greater ranges if the antenna is kept nearly vertical, as is likely in a motor cruiser. The unity gain antenna, about one and a half metres long, has a radiated beam with a wider spread and, as it's less likely to be affected by heeling, is recommended for sailing yachts.

Ideally, the full power available from the transmitter should be radiated from the antenna but there will always be some loss in the feeder cable. Use the best quality low loss cable from the radiotelephone to the antenna and keep the number of connectors or joins to a minimum.

The propagation of VHF radio waves is little more than line-of-sight so antenna height is very important. It's normally positioned at the masthead, lower down it may be masked by the rigging, making communication difficult on certain relative bearings. A secondary, portable hand-held antenna will be invaluable on the day the rig is lost in a gale.

Care should be taken to avoid running the antenna feeder cable near other cables feeding sensitive equipment such as wind instruments, logs and electronic self steering equipment. Even low loss cable will radiate.

Radio waves can be affected by various factors. High barometric pressure or increased humidity often give greater ranges than normal. Rough seas, causing the ship's antenna to sway back and forth, cause 'fluttering' and reduce the range considerably.

VHF EQUIPMENT

Features on VHF radios

Alpha-numeric keypad

On/off and volume

Radio screen
Channel 16 selected

Distress button
beneath sliding
panel

Ch 16 over-ride

Squelch
control

Transmitted power
1 or 25 watts

'Enter' button used
to send all DSC
alerts other than
distress

Fist microphone with
press-to-transmit switch

Fig 4.1

On/off control and volume
This set has a combined on/off and volume control.

Squelch control
Reception is often accompanied by a background hiss; adjusting the squelch control will reduce the noise to acceptable levels. Be careful not to turn it up too much or distant and faint transmissions will be lost.

Press to transmit switch
When the press-to-transmit switch is depressed you can speak but not listen. Release it after speaking to hear the reply. This system of transmitting and receiving, called Simplex, is explained on page seven.

Power output
The maximum permitted power output for small craft VHF in the Maritime Band is 25 watts but sets also have a low power output of about 1 watt. Whenever possible, this should be used as it transmits over a much shorter range and is less likely to interfere with other communications on the same frequency. When sets are first switched on 25 watts is automatically selected. Except in an emergency you should change to one watt before transmitting.

Distress button
The red distress button is found on sets fitted with Digital Selective Calling (DSC). It is activated only when the vessel to which it is fitted is in distress and is always protected in some way so that it cannot be activated by accident. If pressed once and then pressed again an audible signal will be heard as it progresses through a five second countdown sequence.

If it detects a DSC alert, your VHF radio immediately tunes to Ch16 and sounds a loud buzzer. DSC is explained in more detail later in the chapter.

Channel 16 over-ride

This button allows Ch16 (the International Distress, Safety and Calling frequency) to be selected without using the alpha-numeric key pad.

Dual watch (often labelled D/W)

Dual watch enables an operator to monitor Ch16 and one other selected channel. The receiver is switched to the selected channel but, when a transmission is detected on Ch16, it automatically switches over, reverting to the selected channel when the transmission ends. This means you can listen to, say, a port operations frequency while monitoring Ch16. Some sets offer triple watch where Ch16 and two other channels can be monitored.

Scanning

Any number of channels can be selected and the receiver listens to each in turn. If it receives a signal it remains on that channel until the transmission ends but if no incoming signal is received in a couple of seconds, it moves to the next selected channel. There is no priority for Ch16 so you cannot be certain that you have not missed an important transmission, particularly if a large number of channels is selected.

DIGITAL SELECTIVE CALLING (DSC)

The addition of DSC equipment to a marine VHF radio completely changes the method of making initial contact with other stations. This book covers Class D, the one usually found in small craft venturing up to 60 miles from a safe haven. All receivers in this class will be similar.

If GPS is interfaced with the DSC Controller, the position of the ship in distress will be included as part of the distress alert, giving sufficient information for a search to start. If GPS is not available, the ship's position should be entered manually at least every four hours. If the position is more than 24 hours old it will revert to a line of 9's on the display and no position will be included in the distress alert.

General features

The DSC Controller is linked to, or is an integral part of, a conventional VHF radio. *Fig 4.1* shows an integrated set; the DSC component of two part equipment is illustrated later in the chapter. Just like a radio pager, the DSC Controller/Radio alerts another radio that it is being called and tells us that we must go to the radio to contact the caller. Thereafter the system is used like a conventional VHF radio.

A Distress Alert and an All-Ships call can always be sent, but to make a call to a specific ship or shore radio using your DSC Controller you must first know two things:

1. that the station to be called is fitted with DSC.
2. its Maritime Mobile Service Identity (MMSI).

Maritime mobile service identity (MMSI)

An MMSI is a unique nine digit number that identifies a particular ship or shore station. Those for ship stations are issued free of charge by the licensing authority and entered into the set on purchase. Each MMSI contains the country code, UK vessels being identified with the numbers 232, 233, 234 or 235.

Coast Station MMSIs are often published in nautical almanacs and a searchable list of ship stations is kept by the International Telecommunication Union on their website: www.itu.int/MARS/.

If the vessel you wish to call is not listed you will need to obtain the MMSI from the boat owner.

There are four types of MMSI:

a) Ship station
b) Coast station (usually a Maritime Rescue Centre)
c) Group station (programmable by the user. Number allocated by Ofcom)
d) Portable DSC equipment

All contain nine digits but group and coast station numbers start with either one or two zeros to distinguish them from ship stations. Hand held VHF/DSC sets are allocated a modified ship station MMSI. The digits 2359 identify UK portable equipment. For example:

M/V Abbotsgrange	UK Ship Station	232003556
Solent Coastguard	UK Coast Station	002320011
Nonsuch Yacht Charters	UK Group	023207823
Crosma Joburg	French Coast Station	002275200
M/V Bagot	Dutch Ship Station	244005297
Ten Islands Race	Eire Group	025000927
———	UK Portable DSC	235900498

DSC features

The Menu System

To use the DSC for anything other than a distress call it is necessary to understand the menu system, the information interface and guide to which will be found on the screen. Different manufacturers produce different layouts but they all provide similar functions which must conform to the specification for a Class D DSC Controller. *Fig 4.2* shows a typical menu.

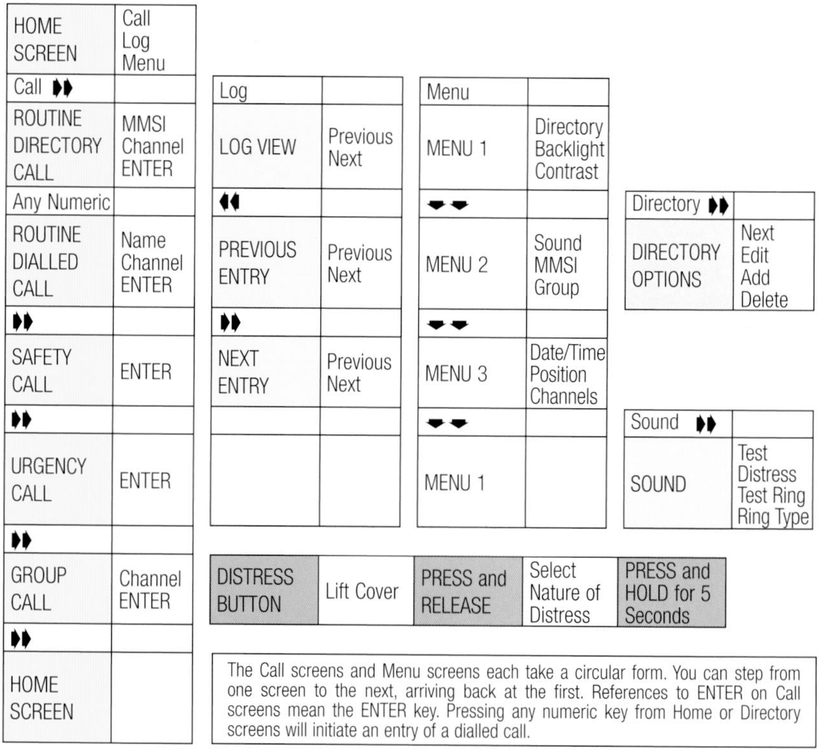

Call screens

HOME SCREEN	Call Log Menu
Call ▶▶	
ROUTINE DIRECTORY CALL	MMSI Channel ENTER
Any Numeric	
ROUTINE DIALLED CALL	Name Channel ENTER
▶▶	
SAFETY CALL	ENTER
▶▶	
URGENCY CALL	ENTER
▶▶	
GROUP CALL	Channel ENTER
▶▶	
HOME SCREEN	

Log

Log	
LOG VIEW	Previous Next
◀◀	
PREVIOUS ENTRY	Previous Next
▶▶	
NEXT ENTRY	Previous Next

Menu

Menu	
MENU 1	Directory Backlight Contrast
▼ ▼	
MENU 2	Sound MMSI Group
▼ ▼	
MENU 3	Date/Time Position Channels
▼ ▼	
MENU 1	

Directory ▶▶

Directory ▶▶	
DIRECTORY OPTIONS	Next Edit Add Delete

Sound ▶▶

Sound ▶▶	
SOUND	Test Distress Test Ring Ring Type

DISTRESS BUTTON	Lift Cover	PRESS and RELEASE	Select Nature of Distress	PRESS and HOLD for 5 Seconds

The Call screens and Menu screens each take a circular form. You can step from one screen to the next, arriving back at the first. References to ENTER on Call screens mean the ENTER key. Pressing any numeric key from Home or Directory screens will initiate an entry of a dialled call.

Fig 4.2

DSC Functions

Basic Mode

Fig 4.3 shows the DSC in basic mode with the Home Screen displayed. The equipment is listening for an alert on Ch 70; the screen gives time, channel and the position taken from the GPS. The main menu and the log of incoming calls is accessed from this screen.

Fig 4.3

Menu 1 *(see Fig 4.2)*   **Menu 2**   **Menu 3**

Fig 4.4   *Fig 4.5*   *Fig 4.6*

Incoming routine calls

This routine incoming call is from a UK Ship Station.

The call is acknowledged digitally when the top button is pressed. Voice communication can then begin.

If the name of the calling vessel is stored in the directory, both the name and MMSI would be shown.

Fig 4.7

Editing the directory

The directory may be amended using the alpha-numeric keypad. Programming is similar to a mobile phone.

Entering Group MMSI

The black line shows a group number that has just been entered into the group directory using the keypad. Note that this make of equipment always pre-enters the initial zero.

Fig 4.8

NAVTEX

Navtex is a component of the GMDSS that displays or prints weather data, navigational information and other safety messages. The receiver (*Fig 5.1*) is usually mounted near the chart table and, as it currently uses medium frequencies 518KHz and 490KHz, there is no advantage in mounting the antenna at height; the stern pulpit or wheelhouse side are ideal. Depending on conditions, signals can be received at distances up to 300 miles from a number of world-wide transmitters.

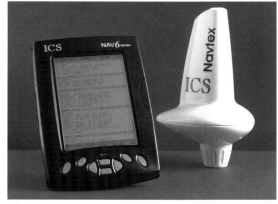

Fig 5.1

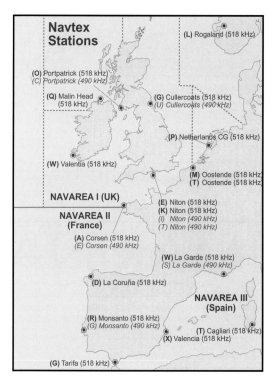

Navtex Stations

(L) Rogaland (518 kHz)

(O) Portpatrick (518 kHz)
(C) Portpatrick (490 kHz)

(Q) Malin Head (518 kHz)

(G) Cullercoats (518 kHz)
(U) Cullercoats (490 kHz)

(P) Netherlands CG (518 kHz)

(W) Valentia (518 kHz)

(M) Oostende (518 kHz)
(T) Oostende (518 kHz)

NAVAREA I (UK)

(E) Niton (518 kHz)
(K) Niton (518 kHz)
(I) Niton (490 kHz)
(T) Niton (490 kHz)

NAVAREA II (France)

(A) Corsen (518 kHz)
(E) Corsen (490 kHz)

(W) La Garde (518 kHz)
(S) La Garde (490 kHz)

(D) La Coruña (518 kHz)

NAVAREA III (Spain)

(R) Monsanto (518 kHz)
(G) Monsanto (490 kHz)

(T) Cagliari (518 kHz)
(X) Valencia (518 kHz)

(G) Tarifa (518 kHz)

Fig 5.2

Fig 5.2 shows the location of Navtex stations in Western Europe and The Mediterranean. To avoid interference between stations using the same frequency they are each given a time slot for transmission. Each station has an identity letter (*Fig 5.3*) and the receiver can be programmed to accept only those of interest - if you are sailing off the English coast you may not wish to receive Dutch or French stations within range. The messages are divided into categories (*Fig 5.4*) and given identity letters so the user can also exclude unwanted messages such as ice alerts and Loran C.

Navtex coverage abroad

Selected Navtex stations in Metareas I to III, with their identity codes and transmission times are listed below. Times of weather messages are shown in **bold**. Gale warnings are usually transmittd 4 hourly.

METAREA I (Co-ordinator – UK)		Transmission times (UT)					
K – **Niton** (Note 1)	0140	0540	0940	1340	1740	2140
T – Niton (Note 2)	0310	**0710**	1110	1510	**1910**	2310
W – **Valentia**, Eire	0340	**0740**	**1140**	1540	**1940**	**2340**
Q – **Malin Head**, Eire	0240	**0640**	**1040**	1440	**1840**	**2240**
P – **Netherlands CG**, Den Helder	**0230**	0630	1030	**1430**	1830	2230
M – **Oostende**, Belgium (Note 3)	0200	0600	1000	1400	1800	2200
T – **Oostende**, Belgium (Note 4)	0310	**0710**	1110	1510	**1910**	2310
L – **Rogaland**, Norway	**0150**	0550	0950	1350	1750	2150

Note 1   In English, no weather; only Nav warnings for the French coast from Cap Gris Nez to Île de Bréhat.
     2   In French, weather info (and Nav warnings) for sea areas Humber to Ouessant (Plymouth).
     3   No weather information, only Nav warnings for NavArea Juliett.
     4   Forecasts and strong wind warnings for Thames and Dover, plus nav info for the Belgian coast.

METAREA II (Co-ordinator – France)						
A – **Corsen**, Le Stiff, France	**0000**	0400	0800	**1200**	1600	2000
E – Corsen, Le Stiff, France (In French)	0040	0440	0840	1240	1640	2040
D – **Coruña**, Spain	0030	0430	**0830**	1230	1630	**2030**
R – **Monsanto**, Portugal	**0250**	**0650**	**1050**	**1450**	**1850**	**2250**
G – Monsanto, Portugal (In Portuguese)	0100	0500	0900	1300	1700	2100
F – **Horta**, Açores, Portugal	**0050**	**0450**	**0850**	**1250**	**1650**	**2050**
J – Horta, Açores, Portugal (In Portuguese)	0120	0520	0920	1320	1720	2120
G – **Tarifa**, Spain (English & Spanish)	0100	0500	**0900**	1300	1700	**2100**
I – **Las Palmas**, Islas Canarias, Spain	0120	0520	**0920**	**1320**	**1720**	2120

METAREA III (Co-ordinator – Spain)						
X – **Valencia**, Spain (English & Spanish)	0350	**0750**	1150	1550	**1950**	2350
W – **La Garde**, (Toulon), France	0340	0740	**1140**	1540	1940	**2340**
S – La Garde, (Toulon), France (In French)	0300	0700	1100	1500	1900	2300
T – **Cagliari**, Sardinia, Italy	0310	**0710**	1110	1510	**1910**	2310

Fig 5.3

All stations transmit in English and some use a different frequency to transmit in the local language. Some Navtex receivers can be interfaced with GPS to print out the ship's position at a selected interval, say hourly. Very useful, when all the crew are needed on deck just as the log is due to be read.

Navtex Message Categories

A*   Navigational warnings
B*   Meteorological warnings
C   Ice reports
D   SAR info and Piracy attack warnings
E   Weather forecasts
F   Pilot service
H   Loran-C
J   Satellite navigation
K   Other electronic Navaids

L   Subfacts and Gunfacts for the UK
V   Amplifying navigation warnings initially sent under A; plus weekly oil and gas rig moves
W-Y Special service - trial allocation
Z   No messages on hand at scheduled time

G,I and M-U are not at present allocated

* These categories cannot be rejected by the receiver.

Fig 5.4

EMERGENCY RADIO EQUIPMENT

EMERGENCY POSITION INDICATING RADIO BEACONS (EPIRBs)

An EPIRB is portable, battery operated, waterproof and buoyant. It transmits a distress alert and allows search and rescue (SAR) organisations to pinpoint the position of survivors.

For all practical purposes there are three types of EPIRB available to the small boat owner. (The 1.6 GHz INMARSAT is outside the scope of this book)

VHF 121.5MHz only

Most often used as personal beacons so that rescue craft can home in on the transmission using VHF direction finding equipment. COSPAS/SARSAT satellites monitor the 121.5 (*Fig.5.5*) frequency but cannot store the EPIRB signal – they simply retransmit it when received. This means that the satellite must be able to detect the beacon and be over a receiver on the ground, a condition called 'mutual visibility'. Because most receivers are in the Northern Hemisphere, a satellite may not be able to retransmit your signal if you get into trouble in the Southern Hemisphere or in mid-ocean.

121.5MHz will be phased out as a distress alerting frequency from 1 February 2009. From that date it will be used for homing purposes only.

Fig 5.5

Fig 5.6

406.025MHz with 121.5MHz

The 406 (*Fig.5.6*) is more useful to anyone venturing further offshore. The search and rescue satellites listen to and store the emergency message until they are over a ground station, making it possible to provide worldwide coverage. The 406 also has an embedded code which contains the vessel's identification number. The precision and power of the transmitted signal, which includes 121.5MHz as a homing device, allows the satellite to calculate the position of the beacon to within a two-mile radius.

406.025MHz with GPS

A 406MHz EPIRB (*Fig 5.7*) has been designed with an integral miniature GPS which transmits current position and further enhances its lifesaving capabilities. When the beacon is activated in an emergency this positional information is incorporated into the distress message it transmits. GPS EPIRBs can fix the position to within 25 metres, a great improvement in accuracy.

Fig 5.7

When installing a 406MHz EPIRB it is essential to inform the Coastguard of the beacon identity and details of the craft in which it is fitted. This information can be given on the Ship Licence application form.

Careful thought must be given to the installation of the EPIRB. It may be on deck attached by hydrostatic release or in the wheelhouse where it can easily be thrown overboard. In either case it must be protected from inadvertent release and inquisitive fingers. If it is inadvertently activated you must inform the nearest Coastguard as soon as possible giving details of the beacon and await permission to switch off. This must not be done until the rescue authorities have been contacted, otherwise a search may continue for many hours to locate the source of the transmission.

SEARCH AND RESCUE TRANSPONDER (SART)

The SART is a small battery operated beacon (*Fig 5.9*) that produces a distinctive echo on any 3cm radar display. Activated in a small liferaft, surface rescue craft will pick up a contact about five miles away and an aircraft flying at 3000 feet at up to 30 miles. It is used as a homing aid for SAR organisations rather than a means of providing an initial alert so can be considered as complementary to an EPIRB. The battery life is about 96 hours.

If the SART is switched on by accident you must inform the Coastguard without delay in case a passing ship has observed the transponder echo and commenced a search.

MOBILE PHONES

Most mobile phone networks are designed for use on land but they can give coverage of up to five miles or more in coastal waters. A mobile phone can be a useful means of communicating from on board now that UK Coast Radio Stations no longer offer a ship to shore link call service.

Fig 5.9

Within the coverage area it can be used to alert the emergency services, including the coastguard (999/112). However, it cannot perform many of the functions of a marine band radio such as monitoring a distress frequency. It can only communicate with a single station so calls can't be heard by nearby craft who may be able to assist, and the rescue services cannot direction find from the signal. For these reasons it is not the favoured method for distress working.

WHAT TO SAY AND HOW TO SAY IT

Procedure cards

Everyone on board a boat should know how to operate the radio and should be capable of sending a distress message.

Ships and fishing vessels required by law to fit radiotelephones are also required to display cards in full view of the radio operator's position, setting out the Distress, Urgency and Safety message procedures. Yachts, which are voluntary fit, are not bound to display these cards, but in an emergency, the lives of survivors may depend on the ability of anyone on board to send a distress message correctly. Similarly, any member of the crew may receive a Distress, Urgency or Safety call and lives may depend on the correct action being taken.

On most VHF sets the operator must press a switch in the handset to speak and release it to listen. Lives have been lost because an untrained operator was unaware of this. A card should be placed near the set explaining in the simplest terms how to call for help.

Since nearly every set has different controls it is almost a question of labelling everything and writing an 'idiot's guide'.

If an inexperienced operator has to bend down to read the little slogan above each knob during an emergency, then it's probably too late. Work out the simplest method of organising Procedure Cards for your vessel. Examples are given in Annex B on page 36.

If the radio is fitted with dual watch, there is a danger of assuming that it is switched to Ch16 because Ch16 traffic is being received. There have been instances of distress messages not being transmitted on Ch16 because the operator wrongly assumed that the set was switched to that frequency. You must make a positive check before sending the distress call. Many sets are fitted with a red Ch16 button, which, when pressed, ensures that the radio is on Ch16 and ready to send.

Standard procedure

English is one of the recognised international languages of radiotelephony, but accents and interference can make words difficult to distinguish and understand. Standard procedure provides a common pattern understood by radio-operators world-wide. Standard words or phrases, used in an anticipated order are much easier to discern against background interference. Departure from the standard procedure can create confusion, reducing the reliability and speed of communication. The correct procedure is well worth learning.

TRANSMISSION RULES ON MARITIME FREQUENCIES

The following simple rules are essential and, in most cases, required to conform to international rules of conduct.

The following are strictly forbidden:

1. Transmissions which have not been authorised by the skipper or person in charge of the ship.

2. Operation of a radiotelephone by unauthorised persons. Passengers or other members of the crew may make radiotelephone calls under the supervision of the holder of an Authority to Operate.

3. The transmission or circulation of false or deceptive distress, safety or identification signals.

4. Transmissions made without identification, i.e. without ship's name or call-sign.

5. The use of personal names or other unauthorised identification in lieu of ship's name or call-sign.

6. Closing down a radiotelephone before finishing all operations resulting from a distress call, urgency or safety signal.

7. Broadcasting messages, music or programmes. 'Broadcast' means to transmit (without a reply being expected) information intended for reception by another person or persons. (Broadcasting urgency or safety messages to All Ships is the exception).

8. Making unnecessary transmissions or transmitting superfluous signals. (This includes chatting about the latest football scores)

9. The transmission of profane, indecent or obscene language.

10. The use of frequencies or channels other than those covered by the ship's licence.

11. The broadcast of messages intended for reception of addresses on shore. (If you have a VHF scanner installed in your home you cannot 'broadcast' to your wife that you will be home for lunch at 1300)

Secrecy of correspondence

Anyone who becomes acquainted with the contents of radiotelephone calls is legally bound to preserve the secrecy of correspondence. No one shall divulge the contents, or even the existence, of correspondence transmitted, received or intercepted by a radio station.

Avoidance of interference

Before transmitting, check the frequency or channel to make sure that your transmission will not interfere with any other communications already in progress. If the frequency is occupied, wait for a break before transmitting.

Use of the radiotelephone when in port

In UK harbours and estuaries inter-ship communication is permitted only on matters relating to safety. Generally a radiotelephone may be used only for port operations service communications and on private channels (eg Ch M2).

Control of communications

Inter-ship: The ship which is called, controls communication. This is still the case with DSC although it is helpful if the operator originating a call checks which inter-ship channels are not in use. He can then initiate the call using a free working channel. The called station may suggest a change of channel if necessary.

VOICE TECHNIQUE

The necessity for clear speech on a radiotelephone cannot be stressed too much. If a message cannot be understood it is useless. Almost anyone can learn to be a good operator by following a few simple rules.

Pitch

The voice should be pitched slightly higher than for normal conversation. Avoid dropping the pitch at the end of a word or phrase.

Volume

Hold the microphone about five cms from the mouth, speak directly into it at normal conversation level. Depress the press to-transmit switch and speak clearly. Words with weak syllables should be emphasised (eg tower, badly pronounced, could sound like tar). Anyone with a particularly strong accent must make their pronunciation as clear and understandable as possible.

Speech rate

Average reading speed is 250 words a minute, average writing speed is 20. Messages which have to be written down (copied) by the receiving station should be sent slowly, spoken in natural phrases with a pause at the end of each phrase to allow time for it to be written down.

STANDARD PHONETIC ALPHABET

An international committee published the phonetic alphabet shown in Annex A (page 34) as the most suitable for pronunciation by operators of many different nationalities, languages and accents. It is recommended by the ITU for use on maritime mobile bands.

If you use your radio infrequently, have the phonetic alphabet exhibited near the set.

Difficult words, or groups of letters within the message may be spelled using the phonetic alphabet. Precede this with the words 'I SPELL'. If the word is pronounceable, it should be included both before and after spelling:

'Intend anchoring off Youghal - I spell - Yankee Oscar Uniform Golf Hotel Alfa Lima - Youghal'

If a Coast Station asks for your International Callsign which is MBDD, you would transmit:

'My callsign is Mike Bravo Delta Delta.'

Phonetic numerals

The phonetic pronunciation given in Annex A should be used when numerals are transmitted.

PROCEDURE WORDS (PROWORDS)

Prowords might be described as those the professionals use. All are designed for easy international understanding and brevity. Not included are such rambling pieces of chat as, 'I am signing off this channel now but will listen for any further transmissions from you!'

The Standard Marine Navigational Vocabulary (M. 1252)

The Standard Marine Navigational Vocabulary was compiled to standardise communication for navigation at sea, in port approaches, waterways and harbours. It sets out certain phrases and terms which should be recognised internationally, the more important phrases are set out below along with extracts of the Merchant Shipping Notice M1252 (available from Mercantile Marine Offices, Customs Offices and Harbour Offices). The M notice also contains an excellent Glossary of Terms, you are recommended to obtain a copy.

ALL AFTER - Used after the proword SAY AGAIN to request a repetition of a portion of a message.

ALL BEFORE - Used after the proword SAY AGAIN to request a repetition of a portion of a message.

CORRECT - Reply to a repetition of a message that has been preceded by the prowords READ BACK FOR CHECK, when it has been correctly repeated.

CORRECTION - Spoken during the transmission of a message means - an error has been made in this transmission. Cancel the last word or group. The correct word or group follows.

IN FIGURES - The following numeral or group of numerals are to be written as figures.

I READ BACK - If the receiving station is doubtful about the accuracy of the whole or any part of a message it may repeat it back to the sending station, preceding the repetition with the prowords I READ BACK.

I SAY AGAIN - I am repeating transmission or portion indicated.

I SPELL - I shall spell the next word or group of letters phonetically.

OUT - This is the end of working. The end of work between two stations is indicated by each station adding the word OUT at the end of its last reply.

OVER - The invitation to reply. Note that the phrase OVER AND OUT is never used.

REQUEST RADIO CHECK - Please tell me the strength and the clarity of my transmission.

RECEIVED - Used to acknowledge receipt of a message, i.e. YOUR MESSAGE RECEIVED. In cases of language difficulties, the word ROMEO is used.

SAY AGAIN - Repeat your message or portion referred to i.e. SAY AGAIN ALL AFTER ... SAY AGAIN ADDRESS etc. (Note: This is a typical use of prowords. The word Repeat would be wrong. Repeat is used to emphasise something.)

STATION CALLING - Used when a station receives a call which is intended for it, but is uncertain of the identification of the calling station.

THIS IS - This transmission is from the station whose callsign immediately follows. In cases of language difficulties the abbreviation DE spoken as DELTA ECHO is used.

WAIT - If a called station is unable to accept traffic immediately, it will reply to you with the prowords WAIT ... MINUTES. If the probable duration of the waiting time exceeds 10 minutes the reason for the delay should be given.

WORD AFTER or WORD BEFORE - Used after the proword SAY AGAIN to request a repetition of a portion of a message.

WRONG - Reply to a repetition of a message that has been preceded by the prowords I READ BACK, when it has been incorrectly repeated.

Repetition

If any parts of the message are considered sufficiently important to need safeguarding, use the word REPEAT.   eg. 'YOU WILL LOAD 120 - REPEAT - 120 BOXES LAGER'.

'DO NOT - REPEAT - DO NOT OVERTAKE'.

Distances

Preferably to be expressed in nautical miles or cables (tenths of a mile) otherwise in kilometres or metres, the unit always to be stated.

Numerals

All numerals should be spoken digit by digit.

Example: 50° 12'.4N   001° 27'.7W should be read:

"FIVE ZERO DEGREES ONE TWO DECIMAL FOUR MINUTES NORTH   ZERO ZERO ONE DEGREES TWO SEVEN DECIMAL SEVEN MINUTES WEST".

If reception is bad the numbers should be spelt phonetically as shown in Annex A at the end of this book.

Position

When latitude and longitude are used, these shall be expressed in degrees and minutes (and decimals of a minute if necessary), North or South of the Equator and East or West of Greenwich.

When the position is related to a mark, the mark shall be a well-defined charted object. The bearing shall be in the 360° notation from True North and shall be that of the position FROM the mark.

Examples:

There are salvage operations in position one five degrees three four minutes North six one degrees two one minutes West.

'YOUR POSITION IS ONE THREE SEVEN DEGREES FROM BARR HEAD LIGHTHOUSE TWO DECIMAL FOUR MILES'.

Courses

Always to be expressed in 360° notation from North (true North unless otherwise stated).

Bearings

The bearing of the mark or vessel concerned, is the bearing in the 360° notation from North (true North unless otherwise stated), except in the case of relative bearings.

However, bearings may be either FROM the mark or FROM the vessel. For example:

'PILOT BOAT IS BEARING TWO ONE FIVE DEGREES FROM YOU. YOUR BEARING IS ONE TWO SEVEN DEGREES FROM THE SIGNAL STATION'.

Note: Vessels reporting their position should always quote their bearing FROM the mark.

Speed

To be expressed in knots:

a) without further notation meaning speed through the water or

b) ground speed meaning speed over the ground.

Geographical names

Place names used should be those on the chart or sailing directions in use. Should these not be understood latitude and longitude should be given.

Time

Use the 24 hour clock indicating whether UTC (Universal Time), zone time or local time is being used.

Calling Harbour Authorities

Most harbour authorities monitor several frequencies, Ch16 plus two or more of their own port operations frequencies. Only traffic relating to port operations can be conducted on such frequencies.

These harbour authority frequencies are listed in nautical almanacs and Volume 6 of the Admiralty List of Radio Signals.

Avoid overcrowding Ch16 and, if known, make the initial call on the working frequency of the port authority. Many port authorities will not reply to calls on Ch16.

If a harbour authority operator is monitoring a number of channels he may not know which has been used for a particular call. Calling practice is as follows:

Harwich Harbour Radio - this is Jasmine, Jasmine - on Channel one two - over

The Harwich operator then knows which channel is being used to call him. Note the brevity of the message.

Garbled calls

When a station receives a call but is uncertain for whom it is intended

Example: .....this is Yacht Born Free – over

It must not reply until the call has been repeated and understood.

Unknown calling station

When a station receives a call intended for it, but is uncertain of the name of the calling station, it should reply:

Station calling Barbican - Station calling Barbican - this is Barbican - say again - over

Unanswered calls

Before repeating a call, check the controls on your set - power on, high power selected, volume turned up, squelch turned down and correct channel selected. Continued repeated calls are a frequent source of unnecessary use of a channel and often the result of the calling station being unable to hear the answer to the initial call, either because the set is incorrectly adjusted or the press-to-transmit switch is jammed in the transmit position. Except when sending a distress call, you must wait a minimum of three minutes before repeating a call.

All Ships broadcast

Gale Warnings, Navigational Warnings, Weather Forecasts, etc. are generally broadcast by HM Coastguard and addressed to ALL STATIONS. No reply is to be made to this type of broadcast.

DISTRESS PROCEDURES

DEFINITION OF DISTRESS

The definition of distress in the 1979 Search and Rescue Convention is:

Grave and Imminent Danger to a Person, Ship, Aircraft or Other Vehicle Requiring Immediate Assistance.

DISTRESS is announced using the word **MAYDAY**, derived from the French 'M'aidez', meaning 'Help me'. This prefix must only be used for distress traffic and, except in a distress situation, the word MAYDAY should never be used on the radio even in conversation.

Emergencies that do not fall into the distress category but where an urgent message needs to be passed concerning the safety of a person, ship, aircraft or other vehicle, are URGENCY messages prefixed **PAN-PAN**.

Transmissions concerning the safety of navigation are prefixed **SÉCURITÉ**.

This chapter covers DISTRESS. Urgency and Safety are covered on pages 30-32.

DISTRESS TRANSMISSION

There are three separate parts to a distress transmission:.

A. The DSC Distress Alert
B. The Voice Distress Call
C. The Voice Distress Message

Parts A, B and C are used if DSC is fitted. Parts B and C if it is not.

To send a distress alert

Fig 7.1 shows the display after one press of the RED button and selection of the nature of distress

Fig 7.1

To send a distress alert from the DSC you should:

1. Open (or slide back) the cover of the RED distress button.

2. Press the RED distress button momentarily.

3. Select the Nature of Distress if time allows i.e. fire, sinking, collision etc.

4. Depress the RED button for five seconds or until the apparatus informs you that the alert has been sent.

    The equipment will now automatically send a short electronic data burst on Ch70 giving:

    a) your MMSI
    b) your position (from GPS or manual entry)
    c) time the distress alert was sent
    d) the nature of distress (if selected)

5. The screen will indicate Ch16 as it is automatically tuned in preparation for voice communication; the whole process take about 15 seconds.

6. The VHF DSC apparatus will repeat the distress alert approximately every four minutes until a digital acknowledgement is received on Ch70 or until the originating station cancels the alert. The screen will display the MMSI of the acknowledging station.

7. Wait 15 seconds and then give the voice Distress Call and Message.

The distress call

A distress call has absolute priority over all other transmissions. All stations hearing it must immediately cease any transmissions which could cause interference to the distress traffic. They must then continue to listen on the frequency for the distress message.

Mayday, Mayday, Mayday
This is Yacht Calamity, Calamity, Calamity. MMSI (or call-sign if not DSC fitted)

The distress message

The distress message follows the distress call without a break and should be spoken SLOWLY and CLEARLY. Remember that your rescuer will be trying to write down your position and other details. The Internationally recognised format is:

Mayday Yacht Calamity
Position (in Lat and Long or a true bearing and distance from a prominent charted object)
Nature of distress (fire, sinking, hit a submerged object etc.)
Assistance required
Total number of persons on board (important as it could affect the choice of rescue method)
Other useful information (anything that may assist the rescuer eg: taking to liferaft, person injured, etc.)
Over (awaiting a reply)

The following is an example of a complete voice distress transmission following a DSC distress alert:

Mayday, Mayday, Mayday
This is Yacht Calamity, Calamity, Calamity MMSI 234001234
Mayday Yacht Calamity
My position is 50° 46'N 001° 17'W
Swamped in rough sea and sinking
I require immediate assistance
Five people on board
Abandoning to liferaft
Over

Fig 7.2 Awaiting a digital DSC response

Fig 7.3 Display in receiving vessel

DISTRESS REPLY

In (*Fig 7.4*) Solent Coastguard has given a digital response. Stand by for a voice message.

Having sent the distress message you should receive an immediate reply from the Coastguard or other shore authority, or in mid-ocean from any ship receiving. Those fitted with DSC will receive a digital response before the voice acknowledgement.

Fig 7.4

The voice format is:

Mayday Yacht Calamity, Calamity, Calamity   MMSI 234001234 (if fitted with DSC)
This is Solent Coastguard, Solent Coastguard, Solent Coastguard
Received Mayday
Launching SAR Helicopter
Over

RECEIVING A DISTRESS MESSAGE

The International Regulations state, 'The obligation to accept Distress calls and messages is absolute in the case of every station without distinction, and such messages must be accepted with priority over all other messages, they must be answered and the necessary steps must immediately be taken to give effect to them.'

Class D equipment does not enable you to acknowledge a Mayday and switch off the DSC alerting system in another craft; that requires a Coast Station or a vessel fitted with a Class A or B controller. It is likely that a Coast Station will accept responsibility for the rescue within a very short time and is in an ideal position to help with lifeboats, helicopters and medical aid.

If you hear a Distress Alert and message you should:

1) write down all the distress information and inform your skipper

2) wait a short time to see if a Coast Station acknowledges

If there is no reply to the message after four minutes and the Distress Alert is repeated, you should attempt to send a MAYDAY RELAY. If that's impossible and you have still not heard an acknowledgement then you must send a voice RECEIVED MAYDAY message and proceed to the vessel in distress, while continuing to repeat the Mayday Relay message.

Note that you won't receive a Distress Alert if you are transmitting on VHF when it's sent, because the equipment can either receive or transmit - not both at the same time. This is one reason why the Alert is repeated at four-minute intervals.

Mayday relay procedure

A ship or shore station that learns of a vessel in distress should transmit a Mayday Relay call and message when:

a) the station in distress cannot itself transmit a distress message.

b) sighting a non-radio distress signal (flares, fire, flags or shapes).

c) although not in a position to render assistance, she has heard a distress message which has not been acknowledged.

When a station, not herself in distress, is transmitting a Mayday Relay this fact must be made quite clear. If this is not done, direction-finding bearings might be taken on the station transmitting the relay and assistance could be directed to the wrong position.

Using DCS to send a mayday relay

The Class D VHF DSC has no facility for sending a Mayday Relay Alert so an URGENCY ALERT should be transmitted (see Page 30). This doesn't include a position and won't confuse the situation but it will alert other stations and automatically switch their VHF to Ch16 ready for your Mayday Relay Call and Message.

The mayday call and message

The Mayday Relay Call and message are formatted as follows:

Mayday Relay (repeated three times)
This is (name or callsign of the station making the transmission, spoken three times).
Mayday (Name and MMSI of vessel in distress)
Nature of the distress
Assistance required
Time (optional)
Over

For example, Motor Yacht *Bluebell* has heard a Mayday message from the Yacht *Sinker*. No one has acknowledged after five minutes. *Bluebell* sends a DSC Urgency Alert and then gives the voice follow up on Ch16:

Mayday Relay, Mayday Relay, Mayday Relay
This is Motor Yacht Bluebell, Bluebell, Bluebell, MMSI 233000285
Mayday Yacht Sinker MMSI 232000789
Position 50° 46'N 001° 17'W
Swamped in rough sea and sinking
Require immediate assistance
Five persons on board
Abandoning to liferaft
Over

IMPOSING RADIO SILENCE

The station controlling distress traffic may impose silence. To achieve this it transmits:

Mayday
All Ships, All Ships, All Ships
This is Solent Coastguard, Solent Coastguard, Solent Coastguard
Mayday Sinker
Seelonce Mayday
Time 2144 UTC
Out

The expression **Seelonce Mayday** is reserved for the use of the station controlling distress traffic. No other station may use it.

If any other station close to the incident believes it essential it may also impose silence, but in this case it must use the expression **Seelonce Distress**.

All stations aware of, but not taking part in, distress traffic are forbidden to transmit on the channel being used for distress.

Relaxing radio silence

When distress traffic is being handled on Ch16 all normal communication on the frequency is suspended. As it is also the international calling frequency, delays in normal traffic are inevitable.

When complete silence is no longer considered necessary, the station controlling distress traffic will indicate on Ch16 that restricted working may be resumed for urgent traffic. The word **Prudonce** is used as in the following example:

Mayday
All Stations, All Stations, All Stations
This is Belfast Coastguard, Belfast Coastguard, Belfast Coastguard
Mayday Eclipse
Prudonce, Prudonce
Time 0345 UTC
Out

Cancelling radio silence

When the distress traffic has completely ceased, the station which has controlled the distress traffic must let all stations know that normal working may be resumed. This is done using the expression: **Seelonce Feenee**. For example:

Mayday
All Stations, All Stations, All Stations
This is Dover Coastguard, Dover Coastguard, Dover Coastguard
Mayday Yacht Sinker

Seelonce Feenee
Time 1045 UTC
Out

DIRECTION FINDING

Lifeboats and some Search and Rescue (SAR) aircraft are fitted with direction finding (D/F) receivers and may request a yacht in distress to transmit a signal suitable for direction finding.

A lifeboat going to the assistance of a yacht in distress and wishing to take a D/F bearing would transmit:

Mayday Yacht Blaze
This is Portland Lifeboat
For direction finding purposes request you hold your Press to Transmit button closed for a period of ten seconds followed by your name
Repeat this three times on this frequency
Over

The reply should be:

Mayday
Portland Lifeboat
This is Yacht Blaze
(10 sec transmission)
Yacht Blaze (Repeated three times)
Over

The request for a transmission for D/F may be repeated as the lifeboat closes the vessel in distress.

FALSE ALERTS

Much time and money can be expended searching for a distressed vessel after a false alert. It is essential that the procedure for cancelling a false alert is known and used immediately the mistake is realised.

False VHF DSC distress alert

Allow the alert transmission to complete once. If no aknowledgement is received from another station switch off the DSC equipment to prevent a repeat transmission.
Switch VHF equipment back on and set to Ch16.
Make an All Stations voice broadcast giving ship's name, MMSI and position.
Cancel False Distress and give time.
Confirm that the nearest Coastguard has received your All Stations voice broadcast.
Example:

All Stations, All Stations, All Stations
This is Yacht Dunce, Dunce, Dunce, MMSI 233003765
In position 50° 34'.2 N 002° 28'.1 W
Distress Alert sent in error
Cancel Distress Alert sent at 0245 UTC
Out

406MHz false EPIRB alert

DO NOT switch off the 406 EPIRB beacon.
Report the false alert to the nearest Coastguard, relaying through another station if necessary.
Give the position and serial number of the beacon.
When instructed, switch off the 406 EPIRB.

URGENCY, SAFETY AND COASTGUARD LIAISON

URGENCY MESSAGES

Urgency messages are prefixed with the words **PAN-PAN** repeated three times. This indicates that the vessel or crew have a serious problem but are not in a distress situation. It is often difficult to decide whether to send a MAYDAY or PAN-PAN message.

Consider the definition of Distress: ".....Grave and imminent danger and requires IMMEDIATE ASSISTANCE", anything less may justify an urgency signal.

Examples of Urgency include a boat taking on water, but not yet sinking; an engine failure with no other means of propulsion but some distance from a lee shore; serious injury to a crew member who needs urgent treatment but whose life is not threatened. Remember that an urgency situation can always be upgraded to a distress situation.

Urgency alerting by DSC

Using DSC select Urgency Call and press the Enter button (*Fig 8.1*)

Fig 8.1

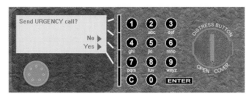

The equipment will ask for confirmation that an Urgency Call is required. (*Fig 8.2*)

Fig 8.2

Fig 8.3

Once it has got the confirmation it will then send the alert and the radio will automatically switch to Ch16. (*Fig 8.3*)

On receipt by an operator in another vessel, the audio alarm will sound and the VHF radio will automatically switch to Ch16. (*Fig 8.4*), the visual display will indicate that an Urgency Call has been received and will display the MMSI of the issuing ship station. Unlike Distress, Urgency Alerts

All Ships urgency
From 234006016
On 16
6/19:47

Fig 8.4

do not include the ship's position (even though this may be displayed on the sender's screen) so it is essential that this is included in the voice urgency message.

The urgency call and message

After sending the DSC alert the operator must wait 15 seconds before sending the voice Urgency Call and message on Ch16. Whether DSC is fitted or not, the voice message is almost identical; the only difference is that the MMSI must be given if DSC is present.

It will be seen from the examples below that the message by voice should be addressed to a particular station or stations. This could be to 'All Ships', 'All Stations' or to a local HM Coastguard Station. Note that if an Urgency Alert has been sent by DSC then the vessel's MMSI must be included in the urgency message to enable the alert and the message to be correlated.

Pan-Pan, Pan-Pan, Pan-Pan
All Ships, All Ships, All Ships
This is (Name or callsign three times)
MMSI
Position, (either lat and long or bearing and distance FROM a charted object)
Nature of urgency
Assistance required
Number of persons on board
Other useful information to assist
Over

An example of such a message is as follows:

Pan-Pan, Pan-Pan, Pan-Pan
Falmouth Coastguard, Falmouth Coastguard, Falmouth Coastguard
This is Motor Yacht Unfortunate, Unfortunate, Unfortunate. MMSI 234001546
My position is 49° 38'.45N 006° 20'.14W
Total engine failure and drifting, my anchor has broken away
I require urgent assistance to clear Traffic Separation Scheme
Two persons on board
Colour of hull black, upperwork white
Over

The nearest Coast Station will normally acknowledge a DSC Urgency Alert and message by voice provided that it is in VHF range. The Coastguard may also repeat the PAN-PAN message on Ch16 after which he will take control of further traffic.

SAFETY

The proword for Safety messages is **SECURITÉ** (French again), pronounced **'say-cure-ee-tay'**.

This word is spoken three times indicating that the station is about to transmit a message containing an important navigational or meteorological warning. It normally originates from a shore authority but may, under special circumstances, be sent by a vessel at sea. This will be a rare event and only likely if you were to sight something like a partly submerged container in an area of high density traffic.

The DSC safety alert

Select Safety Call from the call menu.

Now press the Enter button. The equipment will ask for confirmation that you wish to send a safety alert (*Fig 8.5*) and, when confirmed, will send the alert. Your VHF radio will automatically switch to Ch16.

Fig 8.5

The Safety Alert is less strident than Distress and Urgency. It will be heard on a receiving vessel and by the Coastguard, their visual displays will indicate that a Safety Alert has been received. Receiving stations should be prepared to write down any subsequent message.

The safety call

A Safety Call, given by voice on Ch16 will announce which working channel is to be used for the main body of the message.

Example: on Ch16

Sécurité, Sécurité, Sécurité
All Stations, All Stations, All Stations
This is Humber Coastguard, Humber Coastguard, Humber Coastguard
For urgent navigational warning listen Channel 67
Out

Then on Ch67

Sécurité, Sécurité, Sécurité
All Stations, All Stations, All Stations
This is Humber Coastguard, Humber Coastguard, Humber Coastguard
Large drifting hulk reported in position five one degrees four zero minutes North, one
    degree one zero minutes East
Considered to be a danger to surface navigation
Time of origin one two three zero UTC
Out

All stations hearing the safety call on Ch16 should switch to the working channel (Ch67). They must listen to the message until they are satisfied that it is of no concern to them. They must not make any transmission likely to interfere with the message.

COASTGUARD LIAISON

Calling the coastguard

All HM Coastguard Rescue Centres keep a constant watch on VHF DSC Ch70 and 16. Ch67 is available in the UK for use by small craft and for the exchange of SAFETY information in situations which do not justify the use of distress or urgency procedures.

Urgent medical advice can be obtained through any UK HM Coastguard Maritime Rescue Centre by using an URGENCY DSC ALERT. The voice follow-up on Ch16 should be prefixed with the words PAN-PAN spoken three times. The call and message follows the same format as the Urgency call shown earlier in this chapter.

The Coastguard encourages skippers of small craft on longer passages to pass safety information; who you are and where you are going. However HMCG has neither the facilities nor the manpower to continually track a yacht's progress from port to port and they won't initiate a search unless your shore-side contact informs them that you are overdue.

Meteorological information

As soon as a gale or storm warning is received an announcment is made on Ch16. This announcment will direct listeners to a working channel, typically Ch 10, 23, 73 or 86. Routine weather information is broadcast on the same channels every four hours (after an initial broadcast on Ch16). Part of the National Shipping Forecast (excluding the General Synopsis) is read twice daily together with an inshore forecast and 3 day outlook. For example, Solent Coastguard transmits this informaton at 0840 and 2040 UTC.

In UK coastal waters HM Coastguard broadcasts a local area forecast at four hour intervals. The times of these broadcasts are staggered to avoid interference between stations and are as follows:

MRCC/MRSC (COASTGUARD)	4 hourly (UTC) from	INSHORE WATERS AREAS
Falmouth	0140	Lands End to St David's Head inc Bristol Channel Lyme Regis to Lands End inc Isles of Scilly
Brixham	005	Lyme Regis to Lands End inc Isles of Scilly
Portland	0220	Selsey Bill to Lyme Regis
Solent	0040	Selsey Bill to Lyme Regis
Dover*	0105	North Foreland to Selsey Bill
Thames	0010	The Wash to North Foreland
Yarmouth	0040	The Wash to North Foreland
Humber	0340	Berwick on Tweed to Whitby and Whitby to The Wash
Forth	0205	Rattray Head to Berwick on Tweed
Aberdeen	0320	Cape Wrath to Rattray Head inc Orkney
Shetland	0105	Shetland Island out to 60 miles from Lerwick Cape Wrath to Rattray Head inc Orkney
Stornway	0110	Ardnamurchan Point to Cape Wrath inc the Outer Hebrides
Clyde	0020	Mull of Galloway to Mull of Kintyre inc Firth of Clyde and North Channel. Mull of Kintyre to Ardnamurchan Point
Liverpool	0210	Colwyn Bay to the Mull of Galloway inc Isle of Man
Holyhead	0235	St David's Head to Colwyn Bay inc St George's Channel
Milford Haven	0335	St David's Head to Colwyn Bay inc St George's Channel Lands End to St David's Head inc Bristol Channel
Swansea	0005	Lands End to St David's Head inc Bristol Channel
Belfast	0305	Loch Foyle to Carlingford Loch

*Note: Dover Coastguard also broadcasts weather information on Ch 11 at 4 hourly intervals from 0400 UTC.

Details of European shore stations issuing meteorological bulletins at fixed times are published in nautical almanacs.

VHF direction finding

A number of Coastguard Stations can obtain a radio bearing from a Ch16 transmission. Simultaneous bearings from two or more Coastguard aerial sites will provide a position fix. The primary purpose is to assist in the rescue of casualties but the Coastguard may be able to provide such information to a yachtsman who is concerned about his position. It should be stressed, that this is not an entitlement but a bonus if it happens to be available.

In other European countries Rescue Centres use different working channels and you are advised to consult a good nautical almanac for the relevant information.

FIGURE-SPELLING TABLES

Letter	Word	Pronounced as
A	Alfa	AL FAH
B	Bravo	BRAH VOH
C	Charlie	CHAR LEE or SHAR LEE
D	Delta	DELL TAH
E	Echo	ECK OH
F	Foxtrot	FOKS TROT
G	Golf	GOLF
H	Hotel	HOH TELL
I	India	IN DEE AH
J	Juliet	JEW LEE ETT
K	Kilo	KEY LOH
L	Lima	LEE MAH
M	Mike	MIKE
N	November	NO VEM BER
O	Oscar	OSS CAH
P	Papa	PAH PAH
Q	Quebec	KEH BECK
R	Romeo	ROW ME OH
S	Sierra	SEE AIR RAH
T	Tango	TANG GO
U	Uniform	YOU NEE FORM or OO NEE FORM
V	Victor	VIK TAH
W	Whiskey	WISS KEY
X	X-ray	ECKS RAY
Y	Yankee	YANG KEY
Z	Zulu	ZOO LOO

Note: The syllables to be emphasised are underlined

PHONETIC NUMERALS

When numerals are transmitted by radiotelephone, the following rules for their pronunciation should be observed.

Numeral	Spoken as
1	WUN
2	TOO
3	TREE
4	FOW-ER
5	FIFE
6	SIX
7	SEV-EN
8	AIT
9	NIN-ER
0	ZERO

Numerals should be transmitted digit by digit except that multiples of thousands may be spoken as such.

Numeral	Spoken as
44	FOW-ER FOW-ER
90	NIN-ER ZERO
1478	WUN FOW-ER SEV-EN AIT
7000	SEV-EN THOUSAND
136	WUN TREE SIX
500	FIFE ZERO ZERO

The following procedure card should be displayed in full view of the VHF radio installation (as per instructions given in M Notice 1646).

This Distress Procedure card is for vessels **FITTED WITH DIGITAL SELECTIVE CALLING.** The words printed in bold type should be highlighted in RED.

DISTRESS PROCEDURE

Name of Vessel .... MMSI ....Callsign ....

DISTRESS ALERTS are to be made only when IMMEDIATE ASSISTANCE IS REQUIRED

What you must do:

Check that the main battery is switched on

Switch on the VHF/DSC

Open the cover to the RED distress button

Press the RED button once

If time permits select DISTRESS TYPE i.e. SINKING, FIRE etc.

Press and hold the RED button down for 5 seconds

Wait for 15 seconds then DEPRESS THE TRANSMIT BUTTON on the hand microphone.

Speaking SLOWLY and CLEARLY into the microphone SAY:

MAYDAY, MAYDAY, MAYDAY

THIS IS	(Repeat name of vessel three times)
MMSI	(See above)
MAYDAY	(Name of vessel spoken once)
MY POSITION IS	(Latitude and Longitude or True bearing and distance from a charted feature)
NATURE OF DISTRESS	(e.g. sinking, on fire, etc)

I REQUIRE IMMEDIATE ASSISTANCE

NUMBER OF PERSONS ON BOARD and OTHER USEFUL INFORMATION

OVER

Release the transmit button and wait for an acknowledgement

Keep listening on Ch16 for instructions

If an acknowledgement is not received repeat the voice distress call and message

The following procedure card should be displayed in full view of the VHF radio installation. (as per instructions given in M Notice 1646).

This version is for vessels **NOT** **FITTED WITH DIGITAL SELECTIVE CALLING.**
The words printed in bold type should be highlighted in **RED**

DISTRESS PROCEDURE

Name of Vessel .... Callsign ....

DISTRESS CALLS are to be made only when **IMMEDIATE ASSISTANCE IS REQUIRED**

What you must do:

Check that the main battery is switched on
Switch on the VHF. Check Ch16 25W is selected

DEPRESS THE TRANSMIT BUTTON on the hand microphone.

MAYDAY, MAYDAY, MAYDAY

THIS IS	(Repeat name of vessel three times)
CALLSIGN	(See above)
MAYDAY	(Name of vessel spoken once)
MY POSITION IS	(Latitude and Longitude or True bearing and distance from a charted feature)
NATURE OF DISTRESS	(e.g. sinking, on fire, etc)

I REQUIRE IMMEDIATE ASSISTANCE

NUMBER OF PERSONS ON BOARD and OTHER USEFUL INFORMATION

OVER

Release the transmit button and wait for an acknowledgement
Keep listening on Ch16 for instructions
If an acknowledgement is not received repeat the voice distress call and message

ANNEX C - VHF FREQUENCIES

INTERNATIONAL VHF FREQUENCIES

Channel Number	Notes	Transmitting Frequency MHz		Intership	Port Operations and Ship Movement		Public Correspondence
		Ship Stations	Coast Stations		Single Frequency	Two Frequency	
60		156.025	160.625			X	X
01		156.050	160.650			X	X
61		156.075	160.675			X	X
02		156.100	160.700			X	X
62		156.125	160.725			X	X
03		156.150	160.750			X	X
63		156.175	160.775			X	X
04		156.200	160.800			X	X
64		156.225	160.825			X	X
05		156.250	160.850			X	X
65		156.275	160.875			X	X
06		156.300	156.300	X			
66		156.325	160.925			X	X
07		156.350	160.950			X	X
67		156.375	156.375	Small Ship Safety Channel			
08		156.400	156.400	X			
68		156.425	156.425		X		
09	1	156.450	156.450	X	X		
69	1	156.475	156.475	X	X		
10	1, 4	156.500	156.500	X	X		
70	3	156.525	156.525	Digital Selective Calling Only			
11		156.550	156.550		X		
71		156.575	156.575		X		
12		156.600	156.600		X		
72		156.625	156.625	X			
13	1	156.650	156.650	X	X	Bridge to Bridge Working	
73	1	156.675	156.675	X	X		
14		156.700	156.700		X		
74		156.725	156.725		X		
15	1, 2	156.750	156.750	X	X		

Channel Number	Notes	Transmitting Frequency MHz		Intership	Port Operations and Ship Movement		Public Correspondence
		Ship Stations	Coast Stations		Single Frequency	Two Frequency	
75	5		**156.775**	**Guard Band**			
16		156.800	156.800	Distress Safety and Calling			
76	5		**156.825**	**Guard Band**			
17	1, 2	156.850	156.850	X	X		
77		156.875	156.875	X			
18		156.900	161.500			X	
78		156.925	161.525			X	X
19		156.950	161.550			X	
79		156.975	161.575			X	
20		157.000	161.600			X	
80		157.025	161.625			X	
21		157.050	161.650			X	
81		157.075	161.675			X	X
22		157.100	161.700			X	
82		157.125	161.725			X	X
23	6	157.150	161.750	HM Coastguard Routine Weather & Safety (UK)			
83		157.175	161.775				X
24		157.200	161.800				X
84		157.225	161.825		X		X
25		157.250	161.850				X
85		157.275	161.875				X
26		157.300	161.900				X
86	6	157.325	161.925	HM Coastguard Routine Weather & Safety (UK)			
27		157.350	161.950				X
87		157.375	161.975				X
28		157.400	161.200				X
88		157.425	162.025				X

Notes:

1. Although there are 11 intership channels listed in this International Agreement, in practice only the channels **NOT** shared with Port Operations should be selected for intership use, ie. 06, 08, 72 and 77.

2. Channels 15 and 17 are restricted to 1 watt, the transmitter will automatically switch to low power when these channels are selected.

3. Channel 70 is reserved for Digital Selective Calling and must **NEVER** be used for voice communication.

4. Channel used for Oil Pollution Control.

5. The Guard Band channels cannot be selected on type approved equipment.

6. HMCG also use Ch10 & 73 for routine weather & safety broadcasts.

VHF FREQUENCIES USED IN THE USA

Channel Number	Transmitting Frequency MHz		Use
	Ship Stations	Coast Stations	
15	Nil	156.750	Environmental – receive only
	Nil	156.775	Guard Band – Not Used
	Nil	156.825	Guard Band – Not Used
01A	156.050	156.050	Port Operations (Simplex)
63A	156.175	156.175	Port Operations (Simplex)
05A	156.250	156.250	Port Operations (Simplex)
65A	156.275	156.275	Port Operations (Simplex)
06	156.300	156.300	Intership Safety
66A	156.325	156.325	Port Operations (Simplex)
07A	156.350	156.350	Commercial
67	156.375	156.375	Commercial
08	156.400	156.400	Commercial Intership
68	156.425	156.425	Non Commercial
09	156.450	156.450	Boater Calling
69	156.475	156.475	Non Commercial
10	156.500	156.500	Commercial
70	156.525	156.525	Digital Selective Calling Only
11	156.550	156.550	Commercial
71	156.575	156.575	Non Commercial
12	156.600	156.600	Port Operations (Simplex)
72	156.625	156.625	Non Commercial Intership (Simplex)
13	156.650	156.650	Bride-to-Bridge Safety of Navigation (Simplex)
73	156.675	156.675	Port Operations (Simplex)
14	156.700	156.700	Port Operations (Simplex)
74	156.725	156.725	Port Operations (Simplex)
16	156.800	156.800	Distress, Safety and Calling Only
17	156.850	156.850	State Control
77	156.875	156.875	Port Operations (Simplex)
18A	156.900	156.900	Commercial

Channel Number	Transmitting Frequency MHz		Use
	Ship Stations	Coast Stations	
78A	156.925	156.925	Non Commercial
19A	156.950	156.950	Commercial
79A	156.975	156.975	Commercial
20	157.000	161.600	Port Operations (Duplex)
20A	157.000	157.000	Port Operations (Simplex)
80A	157.025	157.025	Commercial
21A	157.050	157.050	US Coastguard only
81A	157.075	157.075	US Government – Environmental Protection
22A	157.100	157.100	Coastguard Liaison
82A	157.125	157.125	US Government only
23A	157.150	157.150	US Coastguard only
83A	157.175	157.175	US Coastguard only
24	157.200	161.800	Public Correspondence (Duplex)
84	157.225	161.825	Public Correspondence (Duplex)
25	157.250	161.850	Public Correspondence (Duplex)
85	157.275	161.875	Public Correspondence (Duplex)
26	157.300	161.900	Public Correspondence (Duplex)
86	157.325	161.925	Public Correspondence (Duplex)
27	157.350	161.950	Public Correspondence (Duplex)
87	157.375	161.975	Public Correspondence (Duplex)
28	157.400	162.000	Public Correspondence (Duplex)
88	157.425	162.025	Public Correspondence (Duplex)
88A	157.425	157.425	Commercial Intership (Simplex)

Important Note:

The American frequency plan is included to highlight the differences between the American and International configuration. It would be very unwise for a UK resident to purchase an American VHF radio in the USA for use in the UK; it would not be type approved and would be unable to receive and transmit on many of the international channels.

Extract from MARITIME GUIDANCE NOTE MGM 22 (M+F):

Proper Use of VHF Channels at Sea

1. The International Maritime Organisation (IMO) has noted with concern the widespread misuse of VHF channels at sea especially the distress, safety and calling Ch16 (156.8MHz) and 70 (156.525MHz), and channels used for port operations, ship movement services and reporting systems. Although VHF at sea makes an important contribution to navigational safety, its misuse causes serious interference and, in itself, becomes a danger to safety at sea. IMO has asked Member Governments to ensure that VHF channels are used correctly.

2. All users of marine VHF on United Kingdom vessels, and all other vessels in United Kingdom territorial waters and harbours, are therefore reminded, in conformance with international and national legislation, marine VHF apparatus may only be used in accordance with the International Telecommunication Union's (ITU) Radio Regulations. These Regulations specifically prescribe that:

   a) Ch16 may only be used for distress, urgency and very brief safety communications and for calling to establish other communications which should then be concluded on a suitable working channel.

   b) Ch70 may only be used for Digital Selective Calling not oral communication.

   c) On VHF channels allocated to port operations or ship movement services such as VTS, the only messages permitted are restricted to those relating to operational handling, the movement and the safety of ships and to the safety of persons.

   d) All signals must be preceded by an identification, for example the vessel's name or callsign.

   e) The service of every VHF radio telephone station shall be controlled by an operator holding a certificate issued or recognised by the station's controlling administration, normally the vessel's country of registration. Providing the station is so controlled, other persons besides the holder of the certificate may use the equipment.

3. Appendix 1 to this notice consists of notes on guidance on the use of VHF at sea and is an extract from IMO Resolution A.474(XII). Masters, Skippers and Owners are urged to ensure that VHF channels are used in accordance with this guidance.

4. For routine ship-to-ship communications, the following channels have been made available in United Kingdom waters: 6, 8, 72 and 77. Masters, Skippers and Owners are urged to ensure that all ship-to-ship communications working in these waters are confined to these channels, selecting that most appropriate in the light of local conditions at the time. **All other channels are allocated to the Port Operations, Ship Movement or Public Correspondence Services** and may only be used for this purpose.

5. Channel 13 is designated for use on a world-wide basis as a navigation safety communication channel, primarily for intership navigation safety communications. It may also be used for the ship movement and port services subject to the national regulations of the administrations concerned.

6. Typical VHF ranges are contained in the example at Appendix II. It must be noted however that under some circumstances these typical ranges may not be achieved.

7. A Table of Transmitting Frequencies in the band 156 – 174MHz for Stations in the Maritime Mobile Service is shown at Appendix III

> Maritime & Coastguard Agency, Spring Place, 105 Commercial Road
> Southampton, Hampshire SO15 1EG

RYA Note: Appendixes II and III are not included in this publication

APPENDIX I TO MARITIME GUIDANCE NOTE N0. MGN 22 (M+F)

GUIDANCE ON THE USE OF VHF AT SEA

1. Preparation

Before transmitting, think about the subjects which have to be communicated and, if necessary, prepare written notes to avoid unnecessary interruptions and ensure that no valuable time is wasted on a busy channel.

2. Listening

Listen before commencing to transmit to make certain that the channel is not already in use. This will avoid unnecessary and irritating interference.

3. Discipline

VHF equipment should be used correctly and in accordance with the Radio Regulations. The following in particular should be avoided:

a) calling on Channel 16 for purposes other than distress, urgency and very brief safety communications when another calling channel is available;

b) communication on Channel 70 other than for Digital Selective Calling;

c) communications not related to safety and navigation on port operation channels;

d) non-essential transmissions, e.g. needless and superfluous signals and correspondence;

e) transmitting without correct identification;

f) occupation of one particular channel under poor conditions;

g) use of offensive language.

4. Repetition

Repetition of words and phrases should be avoided unless specifically requested by the receiving station.

5. Power reduction

When possible, the lowest transmitter power necessary for satisfactory communication should be used.

6. Communications with shore stations

Instructions given on communication matters by shore stations should be obeyed.

Communications should be carried out on the channel indicated by the shore station. When a change of channel is requested, this should be acknowledged by the ship.

On receiving instructions from a shore station to stop transmitting, no further communications should be made until otherwise notified (the shore station may be receiving distress or safety messages and any other transmissions could cause interference).

7. Communications with other ships

During ship-to-ship communications the ship called should indicate the channel on which further transmissions should take place. The calling ship should acknowledge acceptance before changing channel.

The listening procedure outlined above should be followed before communications are commenced on the chosen channel.

8. Distress communications

Distress calls/messages have absolute priority over all other communications. When hearing them all other transmissions should cease and a listening watch should be kept.

Any distress call/message should be recorded in the ship's log and passed to the master.

On receipt of a distress message, if in the vicinity, immediately acknowledge receipt. If not in the vicinity, allow a short interval of time to elapse before acknowledging receipt of the message in order to permit ships nearer to the distress to do so.

9. Calling

Whenever possible, a working frequency should be used. If a working frequency is not available, Channel 16 may be used, provided it is not occupied by a distress call/message.

In case of difficulty establishing contact with a ship or shore station, allow adequate time before repeating the call. Do not occupy the channel unnecessarily and try another channel.

10. Changing channels

If communications on a channel are unsatisfactory, indicate change of channel and await confirmation.

11. Spelling

If spelling becomes necessary (e.g. descriptive names, call signs, words which could be misunderstood) use the spelling table contained in the International Code of Signals and the Radio Regulations.

12. Addressing

The words 'I' and 'You' should be used prudently. Indicate to whom they refer.

Example:

"Seaship, this is Port Radar, Port Radar, do you have a pilot?"
"Port Radar, this is Seaship, I do have a pilot."

13. Watchkeeping

Ships fitted with VHF equipment should maintain a listening watch on Channel 16 and, where practicable, Channel 13 when at sea.

In certain cases governments may require ships to keep a watch on other channels. concerned.

BOOKING A COURSE OR EXAMINATION

Couses and examinations are available at any RYA Training Centre recognised for Short Range Certificate Training.

For a list of centres visit the RYA website:
www.rya.org.u/training/shorebased/
or tel: 02380 604148

For serving Servicemen, examinations are administered by Service Sailing Associations.

RYA *Membership*

Promoting and Protecting Boating
www.rya.org.uk

RYA Membership

Promoting and Protecting Boating

The RYA is the national
organisation which represents the
interests of everyone who goes
boating for pleasure.

The greater the membership, the louder
our voice when it comes to protecting
members' interests.

Apply for membership today,
and support the RYA, to help
the RYA support you.

Benefits of Membership

- Access to expert advice on all aspects of boating from legal wrangles to training matters
- Special members' discounts on a range of products and services including boat insurance, books, videos and class certificates
- Free issue of certificates of competence, increasingly asked for by everyone from overseas governments to holiday companies, insurance underwriters to boat hirers

- Access to the wide range of RYA publications, including the quarterly magazine
- Third Party insurance for windsurfing members
- Free Internet access with RYA-Online
- Special discounts on AA membership
- Regular offers in RYA Magazine
- ...and much more

Join now - membership form opposite

Join online at www.rya.org.uk

Visit our website for information, advice, members' services and web shop.

1 **Important** To help us comply with Data Protection legislation, please tick *either* Box A or Box B (you must tick Box A to ensure you receive the full benefits of RYA membership). The RYA will not pass your data to third parties.

☐ **A.** I wish to join the RYA and receive future information on member services, benefits (as listed in RYA Magazine and website) and offers.

☐ **B.** I wish to join the RYA but do not wish to receive future information on member services, benefits (as listed in RYA Magazine and website) and offers.

When completed, please send this form to: RYA, RYA House, Ensign Way, Hamble, Southampton, SO31 4YA

2

Title	Forename	Surname	Date of Birth (DD / MM / YY)	Male	Female
1.			DD / MM / YY		
2.			DD / MM / YY		
3.			DD / MM / YY		
4.			DD / MM / YY		

Address

Town   County   Post Code

Evening Telephone   Daytime Telephone

email

Signature: _____   Date: _____

3 **Type of membership required:** *(Tick Box)*

☐ **Personal** Current full annual rate £33 or £30 by Direct Debit

☐ **Under 21** Current full annual rate £11 *(no reduction for Direct Debit)*

☐ **Family*** Current full annual rate £50 or £47 by Direct Debit

* Family Membership: 2 adults plus any under 21s all living at the same address

Please use Direct Debit form overleaf

4 Please tick ONE box to show your main boating interest.

☐ Yacht Racing   ☐ Yacht Cruising
☐ Dinghy Racing   ☐ Dinghy Cruising
☐ Personal Watercraft   ☐ Inland Waterways
☐ Powerboat Racing   ☐ Windsurfing
☐ Motor Boating   ☐ Sportsboats and RIBs

RYA

Instructions to your Bank or Building Society to pay by Direct Debit

Please complete this form and return it to:
Royal Yachting Association, RYA House, Ensign Way, Hamble, Southampton, Hampshire SO31 4YA

DIRECT Debit

To The Manager: _____ Bank/Building Society

Address: _____

_____

Post Code: _____

2. Name(s) of account holder(s)

_____

_____

3. Branch Sort Code

	—		—		

4. Bank or Building Society account number

Banks and Building Societies may not accept Direct Debit instructions for some types of account

Cash, Cheque, Postal Order enclosed £ _____

Made payable to the Royal Yachting Association

077 | **Office use only:** Membership Number Allocated _____

Originators Identification Number

9	5	5	2	1	3

5. RYA Membership Number (For office use only)

_____

6. Instruction to pay your Bank or Building Society

Please pay Royal Yachting Association Direct Debits from the account detailed in this instruction subject to the safeguards assured by The Direct Debit Guarantee.

I understand that this instruction may remain with the Royal Yachting Association and, if so, details will be passed electronically to my Bank/Building Society.

Signature(s) _____

Date _____

Office use / Centre Stamp